NEWSPAPER TAXIS

POETRY
AFTER THE BEATLES

EDITED BY PHIL BOWEN, DAMIAN FURNISS AND DAVID WOOLLEY

SEREN

Seren is the book imprint of
Poetry Wales Press Ltd,
57 Nolton Street, Bridgend, Wales, CF31 3AE

www.serenbooks.com
facebook.com / SerenBooks
Twitter: @SerenBooks

For readings: newspapertaxisbook@gmail.com

ISBN: 978-1-78172-027-1

The publisher acknowledges the financial assistance of the Welsh Books
Council.

Author and editor fees and royalties have been donated to
www.claire-house.org.uk in perpetuity.

Printed by CPI Group (UK) Ltd, Croyden

CONTENTS

YOUNGER THAN TODAY...

EDITORIAL

THE BEATLES MAKE MOST other groups sound easily satisfied or simply trying far too hard. Uniquely balanced, they both mirrored and offset one another, as if seeing their times through the same pair of eyes.

Their beginnings were inauspicious. When Alan Williams booked their first trip to Hamburg in August 1960, they were regarded by peers as the worst group in Liverpool. When they returned from their third visit in December 1962, they were the best. Six months later they were the best in the world.

One can make out a good case for the Rolling Stones – even the Who – but without the Beatles we would have heard of neither. Without Brian Epstein we would never have heard of the Beatles. He didn't create them but he made them happen. Fortune favoured them again when their indefatigable manager was nudged in the direction of George Martin at Parlophone.

Without his input they could hardly have made records of such luminous quality. Anyone today listening to 'She Loves You' for the first time will be amazed how a record so over-laden with platitudes and personal pronouns can sound so casually brilliant. Their seventh LP, *Revolver,* is arguably the best pop record ever made. Even their weakest offering *Beatles for Sale* contains songs as rewarding as 'No Reply', 'I'm a Loser' and 'Eight Days a Week'.

In the next century their social and cultural relevance – both of their times and beyond them – will be pored over by historians and scholars, deeply fascinated by the decade they so dominated. It was a decade that began in black and white, exploded into colour and ended in a darker shade of grey. For this read: 'Love Me Do', 'Lucy in the Sky with Diamonds' and 'Let it Be'.

The continuing relevance of the Beatles could hardly have been more marked than at this year's closing ceremony of the London Olympics, their music providing a prevailing presence and influence, as we watched newspaper taxis nonchalantly circle the arena.

Can poets add anything more to the canon than the group did themselves? Possibly not, but one thing they can do is echo and reinforce the sentiment most lastingly associated with the Beatles – and one expressed so powerfully by W.H. Auden in 'September 1939': "we must love one another or die".

Writing about the Beatles for *The Observer* in 1983, our last great poet Philip Larkin described the ten years from the break-up in 1970 to the murder of John Lennon in 1980, as "a sorry and fragmentary story... never has a whole been greater than its parts".

As usual he knew what he was talking about, but despite this caveat, hopefully the poems assembled here reach some of the more lasting fragments and touch on the most diverse and uplifting parts of what is both an enduring and ultimately life-affirming legacy.

Phil Bowen.

YOUNGER...

GOING TO LIVERPOOL

I am a middle-aged woman
travelling on business
and I'm going to Liverpool,

where I'll take time out
to visit Albert Dock
and the museum

where my youth is preserved.
The fashions I followed,
the songs I knew by heart,

the faces that convulsed
my own into screams
and sobs, they'll all be there.

I'm going to Liverpool,
and it is autumn.
The fields outside Leominster

lie in stubble, the leaves
of Ludlow's trees are jaundiced
and flushed with the fever

that says they're finished.
The ticket collector
said Thank you, Madam.

My daughter's grown up
and my mother's dead,
and between the pages

of the notebook
where I'm writing this
I keep a yellowed ticket

to a match, a picture
of an actor, Edwin Morgan's reply
to my fan letter,

and I'm going to Liverpool
because I'm the kind
that always will.

Sheenagh Pugh

THIS BOY

Called the churchyard the bone orchard,
imitated the choir master by conducting the cats,
stole fruit from the church at harvest time,
called kissing his uncle giving squeakers,
read *Alice in Wonderland* over and over,
shaped like a hairpin, legs propped against a wall.

Aunt Mimi said "the guitar's all very well
John, but you'll never earn your living with it",
brought him up to speak proper, to write
thank you letters, was outraged at his hair.
Rolf Harris said being angry with him was like
trying to punch away a raincloud.

When the Beatles played in New York, not even
a hubcap was reported stolen. He was born
without brakes, this boy who wouldn't wear
his glasses, who dreamt of circling
above Liverpool in a plane, climbing higher
and higher until the city disappeared from sight.

Kim Moore

CARGO CULT

Long before the rasping of the anchor
or the clang of hull on dock

you hear the tempo of the harbour,
the groan of crane and truck

and scrape of hobnail boot. It's night,
a blind-eye-turning darkness, hotter

than a skillet, summer at its height.
You've plodded half a world of water,

hold full of lumber and a crate
of premonitions from Barrett Strong

and Howlin' Wolf, worth their weight
in benzedrine. It won't be long

till white wraiths appear, ragged wads
of cash passing hand to hand

like plague, haggling for the goods
no shop will stock. The bands

without a name will gorge on riffs
and basslines, puzzle over chords

and fingering, the tricky fifths
and augmentations, learning words

that they would never use in school
and fighting over who can bleed

the blues. The alchemy begins; scales
undress, the rhythms interbreed,

shanties that they learned as kids
insinuate themselves in harmony

and rhyme; impenetrable codes
are broken with each change of key.

They'll go from village hall to Savile Row
in less time than it takes to raise

a fire; the opening number of the show
an overture for the closing of the age.

Andy Jackson

FAB FOUR TOUR DEUTSCHLAND: HAMBURG, 1961

"Und now Ladies and Gentlemun, *Der Peedles*!"
The emcee oozes pomade, affecting the hip American,

But the accent twists the name to sound like *needles*,
Or some Teutonic baby's body function.

The bassist begins, nodding to the drummer,
Who flaunts his movie-star good looks: Pete Best,

Grinning as the drums count four. 'Roll Over
Beethoven''s the opener. McCartney's Elvis

Posturing's too shrill, the playing sloppy,
But Lennon, stoned on Romilar, doesn't care.

Mild applause, segue into 'Long Tall Sally…'
One will become a baby-faced billionaire,

One a film producer, one a skewed sort of martyr,
And this one, the drummer, a Liverpool butcher.

David Wojahn

FATE JUKEBOX

He's 54. His marriage
is quicksand. His job
and car graveyard bound.
But he was fresh enough
to be a Hamburg man
at the time of the
Beatles. He knew
the friend of a
needle-thin painter
who took bottles
and smokes backstage.
He threw up beer
next to Stuart Sutcliffe.
He passed a comb
to John Lennon.
Then the fame zeppelin
took off. He was left
to plot his way
through a plain
German life. But
he'd shine in the
cellar nightclubs:
haystack hair, polka-
dot shirt; really
jerk his arms about.
then he met Ursula
with the little boy face.
They came together,
like an A-side
and B-side,
thumb and plectrum,
bullet and gun.

Peter Lane

ON THE CAST IRON SHORE

Liverpool stares out New York
as if the Mersey doesn't end
where it tips into the Irish Sea
but deep veins the Atlantic shale
and throws up in Hudson Bay,

hung up on cotton and slaves
and vinyl the spin-offs of slaves
cut and canned, their grooves
a trade for a jump on the docks
in blue jeans that cry America!

John and Paul on the Cast Iron Shore
Manhattan sand beneath their feet
skimming stones at sheets of tin:
the walls of Jericho come tumbling down
in a din they call America!

America, where even busboys
own swimming pools, the cars
are big as buses, jelly babies
are flavoured a thousand shades,
and babies weaned on the blues.

America, the land Chuck sold to Elvis
and Elvis sold on to the Beatles
and the Beatles sold back to America
with a grin and a tapered-in suit
kicking from the heel of a Chelsea boot

and into America: the lion's mouth
of the Coliseum is ready to roar,
Idlewild has laid out the tongue
of its asphalt carpet, and teens
scent something to sink their teeth in.

America, where Klansmen burn effigies
of the men they're growing into,
where Jesus looks like the men
they'll become, when becoming
more like Jesus is the new religion.

If they have a dream, let's call it
America, where their stories end,
as the story of America has to end,
stalked by a disease there's no cure for,
within you or without you.

Damian Furniss

SO MUCH...

ANNUS MIRABILIS

Sexual intercourse began
In nineteen sixty-three
(Which was rather too late for me) –
Between the end of the *Chatterley* ban
And the Beatles' first LP.

Up until then there'd only been
A sort of bargaining,
A wrangle for a ring,
A shame that started at sixteen
And spread to everything.

Then all at once the quarrel sank:
Everyone felt the same,
And every life became
A brilliant breaking of the bank,
A quite unlosable game.

So life was never better than
In nineteen sixty-three
(Though just too late for me) –
Between the end of the *Chatterley* ban
And the Beatles' first LP.

Philip Larkin

THIRTEEN IN SIXTY-THREE

We were all thirteen in sixty-three.
Profumo and a Russian spy using the same Marylebone mews.
After 'Love Me Do' came 'Please Please Me'.

'From Me to You' soon to be MBE.
The man in the mask. Christine Keeler in the news.
We were all thirteen in sixty-three.

Staying up late with TW3.
Stephen Ward picking up the tab – the Establishment's dues.
'After Love Me Do' came 'Please Please Me'.

Harold Wilson's white heat of technology.
Macmillan in the mud on the grousemoor in his trews.
We were all thirteen in sixty-three.

Jack Kennedy's 'Promised Land' across the sea
From an island full of noises; John Lennon had lit the fuse.
'After Love Me Do' came 'Please Please Me'.

The Shrimp's dress four inches above the knee!
One of the great train robbers on the boat to Santa Cruz.
We were all thirteen in sixty-three.
'After Love Me Do' came 'Please Please Me'.

Phil Bowen

11TH FEBRUARY 1963

The worst winter for decades. In the freeze
some things get lost and I'm not even born,
but think until you're many Februaries
deep in thought with me and find London
on that day as held inside a glacier;
a fissure where two postal districts touch,
its people caught mid-floe, at furniture,
the contents of their stomachs, a stopped watch.
At these pressures the distance has collapsed:
the studio clock winds up over Primrose Hill,
or the poet and her sleeping children crossed
the mile to Abbey Road. This milk bottle
might hold what John'll drink for one last take;
that she'll leave out for when the children wake.

Paul Farley

IT WON'T BE LONG

'With the Beatles', Parlophone, 22nd November 1963

Here comes the sun, though it's November
and half the globe's in darkness still,
a world of black and white though colour's
just around the corner. Mother's ill,
her half-moon face towards the wall,
but father you are cooking curry, Vesta –
where the hearth is – though no-one's
even thought of going to India yet.
What is this shadow? Come together now,
with easy rice, with every good intention,
with navy trim, with matching pillbox hat.
We are with you father in the kitchen,
and we are all together. The day's half-gone,
the moon is up, and mother's coming down
to help you cook. Soon there will be rice
all over the place. Here comes the heat.
It's midday now in Dallas and it won't be long,
stuff you couldn't put a name to all over the place.

Jane Draycott

from THERE ARE AVENUES

Most days now you float with the hours
letting them go where they will
past doors or garden borders
and like the park-lake ducks,
some rain clouds banked above them,
drift about broad spaces
where hisses are stray cats scrapping over lawns,
walked dogs sniff at each other and bark
to know themselves, their places.

Over the fresh-mown reservations,
down avenues of flaky trees,
with almost no memory at all once more
I'm out exploring territories –
or whatever this is when it's at home:
the council houses in Forthlin Road
looking exactly the same
though one of them has been frozen
to a replica with a plaque,
a replica of itself, by fame.

Because to these places, as you were,
we keep coming back and the same old home
is picked out by nothing in particular,
as a matter of fact you're tempted to ask them
what is it with suburban skies
or pavements washed in sun today?
You're tempted to ask how celebrities
changed this nondescriptness –
an avenue's brickwork and green guttering.
Because there seem no differences …

No, it's not that I mean to condemn
this trooping mysteriously by each spot
with the clicking of heels or shutters, with flows
of cash to places money forgot –
a penurious house-front, a street name
altered by nothing but fame.

Peter Robinson

AUTOGRAPHS

I went to Paul's House in Forthlin Road
off ours but at the council end
for his autograph

   and left my book there (because he wasn't home)
   and when I went for it his dad let me in
      to see which book was mine
   and he asked me if Paul had signed it
   and he had
   and his brother was there
   and wasn't he in the Scaffold?
   and I could hear girls giggling outside
   and they were peering in through the nets
   and now they run coach parties to look at the house
   but nobody lets them in
      (I suppose they've moved away – I would)
   and years later, I offered the autograph
      to a girl I'd really fancies for ages
   and she took it
   but she didn't want me

I still have
   Max Jaffa
   Cardinal Heenan
   and two of Gerry and the Pacemakers

Michael Cunningham

THE CLOSEST THING TO PRAYER / SATURDAY NIGHT AND SUNDAY MORNING

some nights disgorging from dance-halls and
street-corner drifting from dockside pubs
we take the motor mechanic-screaming bikes down
roads crystal-clear with amber lighting,
then overlooking the moon-crazy estuary
spidered with shipyard cranes and derricks,
past Salt End jetties and chemical plants
to the all-night café where 'Twist and Shout'
and 'She Loves You' strike the air dumb
vibrating the huge Wurlitzer jukebox and
pinball tables lit up like neon hoardings

drink acrid espresso coffee in Duralex cups
to kill alcohol swirling around the brain,
watching Honda and BSA in formation beneath
the arc of streetlight. Talking trash

then drunk and chasing midnight girls
we pause to see the distant lights of
trawlers throb across the estuary stillness,
off for Iceland or Baltic fishing grounds

and we pause
for a moment
to watch

Andy Darlington

BEATLEMANIA

She hasn't made a telephone call
Since nineteen sixty-four
Now quiet as a browsing library mouse
She mimes to old song lyrics from adolescence
Drops pennies into brand new
And battered subway guitar cases
Younger than grey hair the last scream
Fainted on her lips somewhere
In the middle of Beatlemania

You were never one of my heroes, Paul
I was into cowboys, and cowboys
Didn't play bass guitars
I wasn't jealous, even when my girlfriend
Looked over my shoulder at photographs
Of you on the bedroom wall
Though I hated it everytime she screamed
Especially when the police came
And introduced me to their interrogations,
handcuffs, and saliva snarling dogs
Who were definitely not vegetarian

The first time my girlfriend's decibels
Redecorated the neighbourhood
I thought a demon had opened
The lid of the Dansette
Laryngitis was number one in the
National Health Service charts that year
The year she kissed you
On the lips of a record cover
Cowboys sang songs about
Cowgirls from Colorado

And the girl next door to everyone
Fell in love with fame,
Rock and roll, and your shadow
Was Krakatoa in the time of McCartney
And the multi-promiscuous voice
Reverberated from millions of teenage mouths
Tuneless acapella tongue hearts
That relegated Casanova and Romeo
To a duet of B-sides

Kenny Knight

THE BEATLES IN ELK HORN, IOWA

Two years on from news clips of Russian missiles
heading for Castro's Cuba before getting to me,
The Beatles' 'She Loves You' invaded Elk Horn's
homes like subversive messages from Khrushchev
on our deluxe black and white TVs.

It's 1964 and our small-town school drilled us in
air-raid practices under wooden desks with a terrified
face between the knees and time for alternative dreams:
nuclear death, or English haircuts to shake on
Yeah, Yeah, Yeah and drive all the girls to screams.

We watched them on Ed's all-American Show
altered in the suggestions of such change.
In the moments beyond that need to listen
it was absorbing the same instant of shock that
hit when Clay stole the history of Liston.

How they still startled in clean-cut suits and ties –
harmonies as pure as Country and Western or a hymn.
It was an Iowa revolution from afar
and airwaves would whirl like a Midwestern tornado
to change our landscapes from there and within.

Mike Ferguson

RINGO HATED ONIONS

"It'll be the Palais. No, the Odeon" –
rumours for weeks
and how to bunk off
to queue for tickets?

November. A foggy Friday,
the town snakes around the block
and back again, us huddled in our PVC macs
frost pinching our thighs.

"Do you think we stand a chance?"
"Did you know Ringo hates onions?"
Shirley points to today's front page:
"They all love Jelly Babies."

We stuff our pockets.
Janice bites the heads off
and we pelt the Fab Four.
Ringo catches one of mine,

grins right back at me,
shakes his hair the way he does
'Love Me Do'
this is the night!

Sandra screams so much
she wets her knickers
Brenda Cunliffe gets carried away
by St John's Ambulance, but I

keep my head – first
to the stage door, tunnelling
through the push and shove
he's expecting me –

he winks
asks my name and scrawls
with love – from me to you –
across his picture in the programme.

We'll drink scotch and coke
I'll be introduced to Paul, John and George
it's going like a dream –
I haven't eaten onions for weeks.

Pamela Johnson

THE CAPTAIN OF THE 1964 *TOP OF THE FORM* TEAM

'Do Wah Diddy Diddy', 'Baby Love', 'Oh Pretty Woman'
were in the Top Ten that month, October, and the Beatles
were everywhere else. I can give you the B-side
of the Supremes one. Hang on. 'Come See About Me?'
I lived in a kind of fizzing hope. Gargling
with Vimto. The clever smell of my satchel. Convent girls.
I pulled my hair forward with a steel comb that I blew
like Mick, my lips numb as a two-hour snog.

No snags. The Nile rises in April. Blue and White.
The humming-bird's song is made by its wings, which beat
so fast that they blur in flight. I knew the capitals,
the Kings and Queens, the dates. In class, the white sleeve
of my shirt saluted again and again. "Sir!"… "Correct."
Later, I whooped at the side of my bike, a cowboy,
mounted it running in one jump. I sped down Dyke Hill,
no hands, famous, learning, *dominus domine dominum*.

"Dave Dee Dozy…" try me. Come on. My mother kept my mascot
Gonk
on the TV set for a year. And the photograph. I look
so brainy you'd think I'd just had a bath. The blazer.
The badge. The tie. The first chord of 'A Hard Day's Night'
loud in my head. I ran to the Spinney in my prize shoes,
up Churchill Way, up Nelson Drive, over pink pavements
that girls chalked on, in a blue evening; and I stamped
the pawprints of badgers and skunks in the mud. My country.

I want it back. The captain. The one with all the answers. 'Bzz'.
My name was in red on Lucille Green's jotter. I smiled
as wide as a child who went missing on the way home
from school. The keeny. I say to my stale wife
"Six hits by Dusty Springfield." I say to my boss 'A pint!'
"How can we know the dancer from the dance?" Nobody.
My thick kids wince. "Name the prime Minister of Rhodesia."
My country. "How many florins in a pound?"

Carol Ann Duffy

THE BUTCHER COVER

Stu Rosenberg was five foot two without
his Cuban heels. He'd met 'John' and 'Paul'
at the local synagogue. Their 'Ringo'
was an Irish kid, dyed his red hair jet black,
wore gold rings he'd bought cheap on Canal Street.

They played the convention circuit in Jersey,
most of the girls old enough to remember Wings,
did double bills with Nilsson and Mike McGear.
I heard them at the Meadowlands Hilton, 1982;
if you closed your eyes, Stu could fool you.

He invited me to his room, ordered champagne
for "Harrison in 22". We talked about the day
Lennon was shot, too young to remember JFK.
Then he showed me his prize, bought for a dollar
at a garage sale in Rahway: a real Butcher Cover.

I remember staring at their picture, younger then
than I am now, in their stained doctor's coats,
surrounded by bleeding chunks of meat,
George's hand spearing the head of a plastic doll
like a trophy. It was supposed to be a joke.

The record bosses issued an apology,
rushed them to Publicity. Suppliers were told to pulp;
some got lazy, pasted the new photo to the old sleeve.
Stu could see the image underneath, carefully steamed
the 'clean' one off, to uncover the real thing.

I was only sixteen, Stu a year older. He wanted
to take me to Liverpool, wanted me to meet his mother.
I never did either. My copy of *Yesterday and Today*
is torn where I tried to peel off the cover,
just board beneath. I don't listen to it anymore.

Tamar Yoseloff

489 EAST 11TH, APT. 3C

for Emily

Cabbies dropped us at 14th and Avenue A,
refusing to drive into the neighbourhood.
Roaches crawled on our toothbrushes.
How we loved that apartment.

We'd mimic the whiney voice
of our landlord in his bad black toupee,
the neighborhood men's dreamy rage –
stalking, on the hottest summer evenings,

some potent idea of themselves – the cats'
lewd and pitiable cries. We walked
thirty-five blocks to the Chelsea Theater
for the Beatles double feature,

returning night after night until
we'd been there nineteen times – the man
in the ticket booth never once looked up –
memorized every word of both films

and clowned the parts on the subway home.
Sunk into our busted velvet sofa,
like the fleshy pulp of some great fruit,
we'd spread the map of the world between us,

calculate the distance to everywhere else.
And when you touched my breasts
something in me let go –
the sad work of my childhood over.

Pam Bernard

RINGOISM

INTERVIEWER: Is Ringo the best drummer in the world?
JOHN LENNON: He's not even the best drummer in the Beatles.

Besting Best to become
the backbeat backbone,
behind the skins, The Funny One.

Finger-ringed, matched-grip,
a southpaw on a right hand kit,
no frills fills and a whip-

crack snare, riser-raised
comes the time-shift tempo of 'A Day
in the Life', the tom cascade

flows through 'Tomorrow Never Knows',
on stage a mop-topped metronome
from Cavern's echo to screech filled shows

at Shea, Balboa, the Hollywood Bowl,
to rooftop swansongs on Savile Row,
the solid rock who couldn't roll

to save his life, or play the dots,
no paradiddles or clave high-hats,
but tremendous *feel* for when and what…

So let me introduce to you
the one and only drummer who
brought the shakes and takes to 'Love Me Do'

the chnk chnk chnk to 'Lucy in the Sky'
and a one and a two and a three, four, five,
here's the beat, I'll never pass you by.

John Canfield

FIRST PARTY AT KEN KESEY'S WITH HELL'S ANGELS

Cool black night through the redwoods
cars parked outside in shade
behind the gate, stars dim above
the ravine, a fire burning by the side
porch and a few tired souls hunched over
in black leather jackets. In the huge
wooden house, a yellow chandelier
at 3 AM the blast of loudspeakers
hi-fi Rolling Stones Ray Charles Beatles
Jumping Joe Jackson and twenty youths
dancing to the vibration thru the floor,
a little weed in the bathroom, girls in scarlet
tights, one muscular smooth skinned man
sweating dancing for hours, beer cans
bent littering the yard, a hanged man
sculpture dangling from a high creek branch,
children sleeping softly in their bedroom bunks.
And 4 police cars parked outside the painted
gate, red lights revolving in the leaves.

December, 1965

Allen Ginsberg

JOHN'S ROOM

John Lennon would come stay with us
when things got crazy for him –
he had his own room in our cottage:
in fact we called it 'John's Room'.
He'd call late at night sometimes
and we'd leave the back door open.

John would shamble down next morning
wanting his PG Tips, Woodbines and cornflakes.
We'd go walking by the river,
take day trips to the sea or the hills:
sometimes John would bring his guitar,
play a few songs for Holly and me.
Our kids called him 'Uncle John'.

It was just like he was on leave for a few days
then had to get back to the war.
He'd trudge off to the train station
with his guitar over his shoulder like a rifle –
and we never knew if we'd see him again.

Brian Daldorph

JOHN'S SHIRTS AND SUITS

The look's cool attitude: he fronts a band
a jump ahead of streetwise wannabes
a Dougie Millings grey collarless suit
with velvet piping, each Cuban-heeled Chelsea boot
buffed like a black on black Jag's cellulose:
customised pastel shirts, asymmetry

evident in the rolled point's button down,
no detail copyable, or John's black
Chesterfield suit worn for Ed Sullivan
the red silk lining red as a Coke can.
He's got the edge, gives personality
to a tie's mood: the drugs give him a whack

to psychedelic – Granny Takes A Trip
and Hung On You: thin-rimmed round teashade specs,
relined dragoon coats, revamped military,
quilted Mao jackets, arty paisley,
frilly Liberty print mandarin shirts,
the dandy resurfacing to inflect

hippy with pinstripe jackets, threads from Blades,
a hot pink satin shirt and full-watt tie
escaped from Gatsby, and he's always on
ahead of the next move, that brass button's
ex-London Fire Brigade, that silk jacket
patterned with roses cut from a sari.

The custom-made accessorised or pulled
from Chelsea's acid molecules – John's choice
comes up as mood-board to the Beatles' time,
his satin suit on Sergeant Pepper's lime,
a transient throwaway: the music too
seems tailored to throw colours round his voice.

Jeremy Reed

TWO POEMS CALLED WAREHOUSE

1.

The days when I knocked on doors and ran off
have long since gone, as have the times I queued

to watch films like *The Guns of Navarone*
and *The Dambusters*. Somewhere in there

my dad warned me not to listen to the Beatles:
did I want to end up on drugs? Later,

at the warehouse, I came to be known as
a good worker. I never expected

more than seemed likely: a bunch of mates like
Paul and John, maybe, a few bouncing bombs.

2.

My dad would be shaving by five; I'd shaved
the night before. I'd make us both coffee

and sit in my overall, hands round mug.
We drove to work in silence, more or less;

he was hard of hearing from the steelworks
he'd been made redundant from years before.

In the army he's driven officers
from point A to point B, still had the air

of that driver. When we reached the warehouse,
he'd go to his place and I'd go to mine.

Geoff Hattersley

LIZZY IN THE SKY WITH DIAMONDS

My dad says he was the drummer
who left the Beatles.
I told all my friends,
hugged my pillow excitedly at night.

On my stage of splintered pallets
I was Sergeant Pepper's Lonely Hearts Club Band;
running on rusty oil drums for Mr Kite,
the Hendersons a riff raff of tabby cats,

dreaming of Dad behind me I sang
'Love Me Do' and 'Please Please Me',
pasting the sergeant's cardboard moustache
onto my plastic doll.

Now, I don't care that Dad scraped washboards,
not snares – never sang 'Penny Lane',
but 'Sailing', arms, like canvas,
waving into the Yorkshire wind.

Lizzy Lister

YELLOW SUBMARINE

i.m. Laurie Wack 1961-82

You laughed at the tall men dropping apples
on the heads of the hapless citizens of Pepperland,
turning them to statues. I found this cruel,
preferring the flowers that kept opening like fans

and the cartoon Fab Four adrift in the sea of green,
cracking bad puns in their miraculous submersible.
We both liked the little Nowhere Man with that
affinity of the small and shy for the small and shy.

But the manic Blue Meanies and their glove assassin
made you cover your eyes with your hands and weep.
While I, wide-eyed, gawped at the psychedelia,
you, overwhelmed, eyes shut, soon fell asleep.

I remember the damp wisps of your blonde hair,
your face, flushed and tear-stained in the flickering dark.
Who guessed then that you would die so young?
I sometimes still feel as if you've abandoned me to sleep

while I've had to watch the whole outlandish spectacle
pass by without you. No wonder I'm always nudging
someone to say: "Wake up! You're missing this!
You're missing the story! You're missing the music!"

Amy Wack

STRAWBERRY FIELDS, DEAD MAN'S VALLEY

They come down our road from Penny Lane
press cheeks to bars at Dovedale School
then want to know the way to Strawberry Fields,
and you try to tell them, talking slow and foreign,
pointing, going back over it all again
as it starts to seem an ever harder place to get to.

In the song it says forever, but big blond Billy
is hairless now, and Fred will wince at ulcers,
and Kite was last heard of in another country.
No one seems to know what became of Wendy
or her sisters, and all the rest who span the bottle,
who romped in grass, monkied in the bushes and the trees.

Dead Man's Valley and the Towers – all the places…
Strawberry Fields and Priory Woods, out of bounds
parts you giggled in – jumping walls and fences.
Larking down a lane where phantom pipers blew
on misty nights, swinging skywards from stout
silver branches – whooping – until the old rope snapped.

Billy, it was, who crashed to earth, but Fred
he climbed on stage wailing 'Twist and Shout'
and we all nicked ale from crates, messed with girls
on the golf course after dark. Skinny Linda drunk
with a posh lad whose old man played the cello,
us lying out on grass, Kite saying all the stars were dead.

When Lennon's Julia rolled up in a Butlin's
laundry van, waving one of his big harps
I sucked it at the mirror going: Someone to love…
Jagger-moves came later. James Brown shimmies.
Years on, sat in the Philharmonic, I heard
the gun: a slammed piano lid playing those fatal shots.

You try to say – there's not much to see: they built
on Strawberry Fields, the iron gates are padlocked.
In the song it says forever, but other voices call:
from the Twisted Wheel and the Latin Quarter
and back to Springwood now – mixed emotions.
It's only rock n roll. Maybe. But I like it. Still.

Glyn Wright

A DAY IN THE HOSPITAL

The fog that morning held
like sleep,
my father looked old,
one eye watery, the other patched.

My mother banged her head
as we got into the car:
"How did you do that?" I asked.
"How did I do that?" she said
as I turned the radio on.

And though the news
was rather sad,
I just had to laugh
driving through the smalltalk.

Hospital windows blinked
in the bandaged light.
I thought of you last night.

A crowd of people stood and stared

as I caught them both
mirrored:
he, looking ahead,
upright as a blindman;
she gently guiding,
eyes fixed on his face.

Nobody was really sure if....

the image held
like morning fog,
like sleep
sweet sleep.
Somebody spoke.

Paul Butler

SHE'S LEAVING HOME

She's pouring Tizer
when he hits her,
the glass jolts,
its liquid spills
and fizzes.

She closes her bedroom door
this unordinary Wednesday, leaves
the note she hoped would say more.
They're watching television.

She turns the backdoor key, remembers:
the sound of a bandsaw,
grandfather squinting into the sun,
Vauxhall Viva seats too hot to sit on.
Those dark thunderous Sundays.

The street looks longer, smaller.
From this garden she stole flowers.
Over this wall she scrumped apples.
In this figure-of-eight park
she caught eels in jars.

Suzanne Conway

FOR THE BEATLES

Lived for 3 days on
coffee and bread, pinched
with the hope of getting clear
and over the radio again and
again shrewdly that electronic
track reached into me, yes
hoarsely their voices name it
the euphoric power, and the
badgered, even the mean and
the timid rise like
Japanese water flowers
in that spirit: old
impersonal rewardless "easy"
drum drum drum drum drum
"Love is all you need"

Elaine Feinstein

ALL YOU NEED IS LOVE

They bring their children now
to see us, over the rebuilt bridges.
Something delicate, potent, in the smell
of a child's skin, his hair,
transcends time and reason.

There is joy as well as hurt,
when he tires of our game,
in his well-aimed handful of toys.
It is a phase. There were always
phases, not to be talked about.

A son's first graffito, saying
little but significant of much.
The mass of motorbikes, summonses;
rebellion pushing the clock past midnight;
callers in cars and quiet conversations.

Posters of Paul and John
over a daughter's bed, their music
closeting her away for hours,
"all you need is love" pounding the walls.
Horses; the cavalletti of puberty.

"Grandad," the children say, "come
into the garden and play – and Grandma".
We count slowly up to ten, then
set out in search of them, leave
their favourite places until last,

find precisely what it is we seek.
Asleep now in his mother's warmth,
'Little Black Sambo' fallen to the floor,
they carry him into the car and are
gone with the sun, over safe bridges.

Maurice Rutherford

BEATLES RADIO

Tell me the song of songs
from your white house, blank house
album house.

Nothing but a crate of notes
right for framing the world.

Paperback to taxi to sunshine-led
chronic fugitives in pop.

We listen to you in the bath
that fillip of fun.

The peal of squeals
and intimations of ecstasy.

My daughter in her bubble bright-eyed self
traps the duck like Lady Madonna to her chest.

Defy us to speak of knowing you
although lyrics fashion my form:

An exoskeleton –
its density levelled with
a burden of foreknowing.

A blister-like love this –
Fretted in a time
to sense longing from other lifespans.

Nerys Williams

TO THE UNKNOWN COUPLE

You made that very ordinary thing –
love in a time of war.
        When war-fires cooled,
you spun it over years of rationing,
the two-roomed rented flat, the two-door child;
a time-warp income which would never spring
new windows open, though the air was mild,
and youth had so much youth and peace and 'All
You Need Is Love' –
        but what's that lovely trick
of catching up if you were born
    too soon?

The last dance saved, the dance-steps prove too quick:
he's got dementia, she, arthritis; then
what does it matter there's no cash to spare
for
  first-time cruise or
       second honeymoon?

I want them, though: I owe you all you wish –
who, with the twentieth-century, thinned to ash
without me, with no need of me.
       How long
I've kept those ball-room gloves – even the drawer
they dreamed in, sweet tale-scented like the schmaltz
of Movieland!
    And still I can't come near
your blitz-flushed black-out nights, or see you waltz
into my not-yet life, humming the song
I never heard:
    love in a time of war.

Carol Rumens

CONVERSATION ON A TRAIN

I'm Shirley, she's Mary.
We're from Swansea
(if there was a horse there
it'd be a one-horse town
but it isn't even that).
We're going to Blackpool.
Just the week. A bit late, I know.
But then there's the illuminations
isn't there? No, never been before.
Paris last year. Didn't like it.
Too expensive and nothing there really.

Dirty old train isn't it?
And not even a running buffet.
Packet of crisps would do.
Change at Crewe.
probably have to wait hours
for the connection, and these cases
are bloody heavy.
And those porters only want tipping.
Reminds you of Paris that does.
Tip tip tip all the time.
Think you're made of money over there.

Toy factory, and Mary works in a shop.
Grocers. Oh it's not bad.
Mind you the money's terrible.
Where are you from now?
Oh aye, diya know the Beatles then?
Liar!
And what do you do for a living?
You don't say.
Diya hear that Mary?
Well I hope you don't go home
and write a bloody poem about us.

Roger McGough

YOKO ONO

Yoko's a Fluxus
classical pianist,
she rides a white cloud
like a dance-point pony
it's called inspiration,
and dips over summits,
Mount Fuji, St. Paul's
with its pumpkin-shaped dome
writing in diamond
Nov 6, 1966
a psychic gateway
open at Indica
like a white flower,
John in the centre
his neurons like anthers
taking in their meeting
under 'Ceiling Painting'
a canvas with a minuscule
word on it as a skylight.
White on white pieces,
some are transparent,
the chess set's a mirage
all smart molecules,
the one dab at colour
a Bramley's apple
cidery with autumn
grained in its skin,
positioned on Perspex
like a solitary planet.
He bites the explosive
fermenting juices,
takes a half moon out
chunked from the core.
Love's in the flavour
like a telepathic signal,
sweet, sharp and clear,
roundly salival,

the tree and the apple
got in one bite,
tasting of a Kent orchard
in damp russet sunlight.

Jeremy Reed

CARNIVAL OF LIGHT

The Roundhouse, 28th January 1967

They say the bass was a slap on the pier,
the drums a loop of whoops and a jeer –
that together they had the rhythm of breath.
You ain't heard the truth from me yet –
that's not how it sounded at all –
now, let me set out my stall:
close your eyes, you're in a field,
now open them, how does it feel
to see a city that rose overnight?
You've woken up in a carnival of light.

They say the organ skittered,
in its flame was a flicker
of the music this fire might become.
Like any blaze, it burnt only once.
But that's not how it sounded at all –
I was there, dancing up a squall.
Fold your legs and meditate,
what's in your head's no ache –
it's the inkling of your first insight
that'll burst into a carnival of light.

They say that John pretended to be Paul,
or that John wasn't there at all –
that it was Paul pretending to be John.
By the time it had played, Paul was gone,
saying, "that's not how it sounded at all…"
But I was there, with my ear to the wall.
My girl at the time said "that's nice…"
It was better than the rising of Christ!
In the dark for two days and three nights
to come again in a carnival of light.

Nathaniel Blue

BRIAN EPSTEIN

The curtains drawn all day at Chapel Street
on the residual blues. Last night's rent boy
left burn-marks peppered on the linen sheet.

He makes things happen between John and Paul:
his charm's infectious, and it colours deals.
Managing a rock band seems like long haul,

fielding the tacticals from EMI,
shaping an image – cooky ties and suits:
the limit's ten miles higher than the sky.

The bottle's half empty or it's half full,
a drinker's puzzle: he can't get it right.
The pills are gravity-free in their pull.

Sometimes his eyes are puffed up black and blue
from rough trade reprisals: the money talks,
then boots and knuckles claim an overview.

The night's his hunting ground; an unlit pier,
or West End casino, his jaw rattling
over baccarat or chemin de fer.

His need's for love, when same-sex is a code.
The pimply trick he turned at Leicester Square
had little gestures of camp overload.

The band won't tour: he fears redundancy,
internal fighting. Sometimes things explode
inside his head, and leave no memory.

Chocolate digestives by the bed: the boy
he hoped would stay, left nothing, no address,
just matches, and a used bottle of Joy.

This time it's pills he gambles: live or die?
Their dull eruptions happen in his brain.
His shirt's still on, so too his knotted tie.

Jeremy Reed

FOUND POEM (FROM THE WEB)

there is no narrative sense
only 23 out of 100 people liked it
some scenes are arm-chewingly tedious
my father refused to watch it
which added to its allure
this city has millions of people
but it's got no soul

"please stop talking about the Beatles
half of them are dead anyway"

it's a kind of acid-rock 1967 version
of Bunuel & Dali's *Le Chien Andalou*
but with Come Dancing dancers
I think the whole thing is just a hoot
I have taken a moment to re-evaluate
and decided it's still rubbish
I watched it stoned and thought it was great
it would have been better 59 minutes shorter

"please stop talking about the Beatles
half of them are dead anyway"

I don't see why the movie has to make sense
I have always thought cheese and onion
it is an apparent drive to send up an England
of decaying authority, bad food and anti-climactic
entertainment; a car arrived with six midget wrestlers
all light entertainment is only one step from surrealism
our WI had a mystery tour in blinding fog we
could see squat had no idea where we were

"please stop talking about the Beatles
half of them are dead anyway"

the Beatles saw the end of the 60s lovedream
before anyone else did
PS I think *The Lost World* is a better film
it was clearly ripped off from the Merry Pranksters
class structures and unequal privilege everywhere
and then the music that set us all free
it captured the spirit of the time and exposed
a mainstream audience to a type of experimental
film making that many people would not
otherwise have watched
you can almost smell the patchouli and unwashed feet

"please stop talking about the Beatles
half of them are dead anyway"

David Woolley

ME AND MY MONKEYS

It's a long road from Bangor to Rishikesh
but where there's a will there's a way
so travel the names in your old school atlas –
sucking a hookah on the banks of the Bosphorus –
to take a dip off the ghats of the Ganges,
after George and John, Ginsberg and Gandhi,
the dust of six countries melting away.

You've tasted the salt of the Sea of Marmara,
shared sabzi and sorrow with the thieves of Tehran,
touched the feet of the Bamiyan Buddhas,
trekked the Swat Valley to the ruins of Taxila,
surfed bus roofs over the Punjab of India
shading your lungs with that Afghani black
swapped for your passport in the souk of Herat.

Now the Maharishi's ashram's fallen to jungle:
not a sadhu in sight, no sign of the Beatles,
but for a yogi lost deep in his chillum
and a combo of monkeys howling out jingles
from the verandah of Bill's old bungalow
banging on bean cans to work up a rhythm
the Himalaya listening, ears clean as snow.

Damian Furniss

THE WHITE POEM

Rupert Loydell

WHITE

Rather than the *White Album*
it was the *Great White Wonder*
In 1969 I couldn't understand why
the world didn't just go on making more
money instead of trying to end itself in fire

rolled marbles under the hooves of
horses Pentagon surrounded with flowers
kept heading on and higher
om mani padme
roundhouse hum

um then revlt nm um revoil nub rr rev ine
n br in br mthr nnn ure sun son sun
n n bk bk bk bk back t bck in t t
back in the in t tr tr trrr you eee trrr ss
ess ess ess ess bungalow bungalow mk onk ess ss
blu rac n hon hon hon e mmm rus wa wall oo hare dum

started to disbanded Jesus echo snt back har hare
leaving minimal found bed in white suit infatuati
roof plas tur krrr kclap clap crm
wish piece cut piece voice piece arse film
hide until everybody dies

Duchamp as rock star

after that all done

Peter Finch

BECAUSE

I chose 'Because'
because the sky is blue
because it's holy, without God,
because it's hard to choose a track
from that back catalogue that can't
ambush you in a café in Prague
a lift in Orta, a radio at night,
because Chris said you'd liked it,
because they really can sing
because it catches you out
when it stops suddenly –
waits –
then starts again.
Hanging off the bar they all
sang along, had the words, though
most of them were out of it.
Lars looked at me as if
the whole of his life was now
my fault. They'd had black edged cards
with "the first round's on him"
but they kept them, paid anyway.
It was a long afternoon stretching
into dark. Music couldn't save us.
Your choir needed you
to reach bottom E. Pete played
you playing Elvis, got a laugh.
Your boy wore a black hat.
I'd written something, but
when I stood I lost it, because
I chose Because
because I had no idea
because I had to choose something.

Ann Gray

ON THE ROOF OF THE WORLD

'Hey Jude' was the longest single, up to that time,
ever released. It sweats off, chorus like a mantra.
The times are changing. New musics divide the audience
and skirts are longer, but it's a bright London shopping day
when the traffic stops. Only a black cab moves
gingerly through the crowd, like a toy cruiser nudging weed,
and we're all craning upwards: planks and scaffolding
on the townhouse roof and the clipped, drifting music
the Beatles play. It is their last concert,
though nobody knows this. George twangs his Fender, John
hammers-off on his Epiphone, Paul stomps
with his violin-bodied fretless bass and Ringo, dreamed up
by a manager who died a long time ago, kicks the years
out of his bass drum padded with a rug. How sweet

it would have been, someone will write, to watch them
play the Marquee, this funky little rock'n'roll band.
They are so far above us, we can hardly see them.
They are playing for God. They are playing for cameras
because the show's outgrown the road. We can't believe it.
Tomorrow's papers will acclaim a British institution.
I'll read them and imagine I was there like everyone.
They are already going out of fashion. There's nothing left
but acrimony, separation, lawsuits. The last great single,
'The Ballad of John and Yoko', will be John and Paul
alone, hurrying in midsummer heat, the way it was at the start.
Nobody knows this. They have climbed too far to get back
anywhere we might be among the crowd who clap then drift apart
when the helmeted bobbies have the amps turned off.

Lachlan Mackinnon

YOUNGER THAN TODAY...

NEW YORK CITY BLUES

for John Lennon

"You do not cross the road
To step into immortality
An empty street is only the beginning

The words will still flow through you"
Even on this cold pavement,
Are heard in some far place
Remote from flowers or flash-bulbs.

In that city, on Gothic railings
Dark against the snowy park
Still a dead flower, a faded letter,
Already one month old.

'Life is what happens to you
When you're busy making other plans,'
This empty street
Is only the beginning.

Here, in your other city,
Riot vans prowl the December dark,
Remember angry embers of summer,
Familiar ghost guitars echo from stucco terraces.

Meanwhile, in the Valley of Indecision,
We rehearse stale words, store up unexpected songs,
Celebrate sad anniversaries.
Flowers and flash-bulbs. Cold pavements.

"You do not cross the road
To step into immortality
At the dark end of the street
Waits the inevitable stranger."

Adrian Henri

LIVERPOOL ECHO

Pat Hodges kissed you once, although quite shy,
in sixty-two. Small crowds in Matthew Street
endure rain for the echo of a beat,
as if nostalgia means you did not die.

Inside phone-booths loveless ladies cry
on Merseyside. Their faces show defeat.
An ancient jukebox blares out 'Ain't She Sweet'
in Liverpool, which cannot say goodbye.

Here everybody has an anecdote
of how they met you, were the best of mates.
The seagulls circle round a ferry-boat

out on the river, where it's getting late.
Like litter on the water, people float
outside the Cavern in the rain. And wait.

Carol Ann Duffy

THE COLONY

I'm in darkness, 10th floor, Central Park West.
Streaks of city light on this page, bullion from El Dorado.
Chapman murdered Lennon next door. Yoko Ono still lives there
across from her Strawberry Fields Forever.

Almost midnight, rain gusting against my window.
Over there, lights come on, go off, shadowy figures appear,
vanish. In a few minutes, I remember, it will be spring.
The whole city seems to be weeping

for the English boy who sang of love until love twisted
to kill him. On, off, the cells lit, then dark. Now, a single
chamber blooms red, awash with flowers, as though ants had
            dragged
millions of red petals through a tunnel.

William Heyen

IN MY LIFE

for John Lennon

John, John – come on, come on
To what's near and whatever's after –
I hear you're the new Cocky Watchman,
I hear your manic laughter,

Are you amazed at the stars from where you are,
Naked in disbelief?
Been busy making other plans?
Remember what the joker said to the thief

When the same way out means another way in,
Nothing is real and no one to battle –
So clap hands in the cheaper seats!
You others, get your jewellery to rattle –

When there's nothing you can do with what can't be done,
Nothing they say is heads that can't be tails,
Are you seeing yourself as you in time?
Met the boss-man yet with the nails?

John, John – it's ten to one
Ten to nine is the time for a dream –
In a world of cross-eyed fantasy
Slip and slide on the ice of a stream

Of unconscious consciousness,
Bite off what's never been bitten,
See the woman in white on the river at night
Sing the songs you still haven't written

With a guitar from a bar down Mathew Street,
A leather jacket slung on a chair,
The 'one and only' drunk on the bandstand –
This comedian from god knows where –

So shake it up for the girl with the pony-tail,
Shake it down – let it rattle and roll!
Straight from the start with your legs wide apart
And a heart twice the size of your soul,

And John, John – now you've gone
Will the moonlight turn into black?
Have you heard the word on eternity?
Can you see out the front of the back?

And is this what you got for the money?
Click click – what you got for the show ?
Was the bang loud enough? Was there drumming?
Did it come through the quick or the slow?

Because John, John, once upon
A time a rhyme had a reason
And I spy with my little eye
A flaming pie in the briny season,

And this one here's for the Walrus
And the girl who came to stay,
Can you help us out on the chorus?
Come together for the band to play

One more time – feel the rhythm – see the sign
In a glass onion tied in a knot
And I haven't got a clue between me and you
Whether the Devil's in a kettle or the pot

Where Prudence lost her daisy chain,
Maggie May, the key to the cellar,
John, John – second to none –
Such a helluva good-looking fellah –

As made up there as the Liver Bird –
A splash of diamonds flashing by
And John, John – keep shining on!
Above you only sky.

Phil Bowen

THE ASSASSINATION OF JOHN LENNON AS DEPICTED BY THE MADAME TUSSAUD WAX MUSEUM, NIAGARA FALLS, ONTARIO 1987

Smuggled human hair from Mexico
Falls radiant round the waxy O

Of her scream. Shades on, leather coat and pants, Yoko
On her knees – like the famous Kent State photo

Where the girl can't shriek her boyfriend alive, her arms
Windmilling Ohio sky.
                    A pump in John's chest heaves

To mimic death throes. The blood is made of latex.
His glasses: broken on the plastic sidewalk.

A scowling David Chapman, his arms outstretched,
His pistol barrel spiralling fake smoke

In a siren's red wash, completes the composition,
And somewhere background music plays 'Imagine'

Before the tableau darkens. We push a button
To renew the scream.
                    The chest starts up again.

David Wojahn

SGT. PEPPER'S WAX FUNERAL

i.   yellow hyacinth

I step over a red 'B' of flowers
kiss your wax lips
you stand circa sixty-three looking
down into a grave containing
a left-handed Hofner
of yellow hyacinth

I don't want anything here
not even a flower from your bass
just you   but you
are connected to the others
right hand sewn to
Ringo's sad shoulder

I have to get in beside you
shove cardboard Oscar Wilde over
Tom Mix and Marlon Brando domino backward into
Stu Sutcliffe Mae West whoever
the fuck else is back there

I cut your hand free from Ringo's suit
the other pulls easily from your sleeve
drop them to the floor   push
George   John   Ringo forward
into the makeshift grave
they land face down
in dirt their feet broken off
shoes still attached to the floor

it's just you and me now baby
I take a bite from your left cheek
roll the cool wax on my tongue
my left hand inside your trousers
knife hangs at my right side
I swallow the wax lump

let you go
    topple
join your friends

ii. you   decapitated

on the other side of the studio I see
the white Austin Mini on a doll's little knee
outta my way, Marlene Dietrich
move it or lose it, Shirley Temple

this is the car they say you died in, Paul
driving around London at night
nineteen sixty-six, your head
torn free at impact
replaced by a perfect
doppelgänger with a scarred lip
the greatest cover-up in
Rock and Roll History

where did they take your head?
did they preserve it in some chemical
to keep it from decaying?
I'd love to have it but

I'll take the car from this doll's knee
wax ball hot in my gut

step over hyacinth crushed
beneath the weight of wire
bodies wax necks   stiff soft arms

Kimmy Beach

AUTOGRAPH ODE

The street grid sliced the wind that winter, small
surprises at each corner with the knife edge
angles pressing at each turn, a wall:
subzero perpendicular to life
we measured on a warmer scale of fife
notes floating in an acid-head Arcadia –
the Beatles subterranean, nightlife
in hick town downtown cafeteria,
the revolution's bus ride from suburbia.

A script of *Hard Day's Night* with doodled strokes,
the pencilled margins and the corner-pleat,
a souvenir of '64, evokes
the Ipswich Gaumont and the spit-curls sweet
with hormones in a fifteen-shilling seat –
the second performance, eight forty-five,
the audience transfigured in the heat
of chords, suspended on the screams that drive
the middle eight and thrash into the air alive.

The Mersey beat in cut-to-strut drainpipes,
guitars' four-four and stage of scaffold planks
for tinny amps vibrato archetypes
crank up to 'Twist and Shout', the fans' phalanx
as limousines depart: "goodnight, and thanks"
McCartney waves, and thousands stand in dumbshow
desperation, waving back from ranks
that sink, rise sobbing, cresting to a numb
hysteric, the electric canon they become.

The artefacts of travellers recall
an antique time by auction and bequest.
The zebra stripes in Abbey Road marked Paul
for resurrection, barefoot with the blessed
where tapes reversed revealed the alkahest

those cults required. A dream world comes adrift,
and decades fade to standing here. The rest
is feedback, lives sold lot by lot, a sift
through shadows where the psychedelic stars red-shift.

Estill Pollock

RINGO'S ROOM

10 Admiral Grove, The Dingle, Liverpool

great sport, my husband
plodding with me through every
Beatles tour in Liverpool

"this is where Ringo lived, honey
see the doll in the upstairs window?
that was Ringo's room"

"oh yeah?" he says, tired
ready for a beer somewhere
he's finished taking pictures:
me in front of strangers' homes
they peer through blinds as bus after bus
stops before their house
they're just back from work
tired, they'd like to watch some telly
but the constant drone of the buzzer
makes them hang a sign
Please do not ring our doorbell
You cannot come inside to see Ringo's room
It's our daughter's room now

we ride down Penny Lane
in a conspicuous yellow
bus called 'The Magical Mystery Tour'
I've seen it all before
barbershop, bank, roundabout
this church where John met Paul
John's preschool
the children's home hidden
behind iron gates at Strawberry Fields

at the corner of Hope Street and Mount Pleasant
I ride out the last of the drizzly tour
high on Caffrey's Cream Ale
and the stench of sea

my hand on my husband's
thigh nudging
closer as we near our hotel

'please do not disturb' sign on our doorknob
one frilly single bed left empty
as he tries to thrust from me the memory
of tiny British postwar beds
sleepy with dark-haired boys
dreaming guitars

Kimmy Beach

WHEN PAUL McCARTNEY STAYED

Cousin Madge was eating bread and jam
at teatime when a black Mercedes drew
up beside her gate. A famous name
    got out of it, and threw

caution to the wind by taking off
his Raybans. The astonishment was total:
she clutched her temples, for the bulletproof
    car had brought a Beatle

to her Walsall semi. When he pressed
the doorbell, she advanced with overflowing
eagerness to answer it. He said:
    "Hello there, how're you doing?"

Time shrank to nothing. All her tight resolve
    lay useless as a cinder.
The world refused, that minute, to revolve
    as down the path strode Linda,

the singer's wife. Cousin Madge could cope.
Her invitation was assured: "Come in!"
Soon she'd cut some cake, and a best cup
    rose past the well-known chin.

They talked till late. When everything was said
she showed them to their unassuming room:
three plaster ducks, a creaky double bed.
    Linda's ritzy perfume

provided a strange counterpoint. Madge felt
strong as Atlas, wise as Aristotle.
She blurted, "If you want, give me a shout
    for a hot-water bottle."

The home help entered with her master key
next morning. Madge's eyes were bright as flame.
She'd curled up in a corner. Presently
    two paramedics came.

Paul Groves

YES IT IS

It was something to do with the two of us
learning to drive so late; and that collection
of misplaced singles, B-sides, E.P. tracks

and oddities like *'Komm, Gib Mir Deine Hand'*
came with us on our first car trip across country.
The A40. Dennis Potter's road. From Metroland

past Oxford, stopping at Birdlip to glimpse blue
remembered hills, picnicking in the Forest of Dean,
then down through valley-heads to my parents' home.

There were moments of terror: an articulated
lorry pulling into our lane just as we passed
its tail-gate; and anxieties about direction,

and moments of dreadful fatigue. The boys
counted legs of pub signs. And the tape helped:
the early songs most. Ringo's 'Matchbox'

holding his nose, *jealous* rhyming with *as well as*
over a repeated rhythmic chord, and then
that song nobody quite recalled, as if it had been

lying in wait for our early middle age.
Three-part harmony. John and George
obliterating Paul, Liverpool masking Detroit.

Red and blue and the unspoken black,
as Lennon's voice splintered in the bridge,
mourning his mother as you mourned yours.

Tim Dooley

ANTENATAL

Sometimes when your fingers stray
into my mouth it hits me, a sudden
memory of swimming in the saline
Martian dark. Maybe eight months gone,
I float in Rothko roundness, rub up
along her copper-seven, against all odds,
an accident. I'm comfortable there
with my fists bumping my gums;
there's nicotine, and alcohol
in psychedelic bands, subtly
altering cell structures, the flicker
of synapses.
       Maybe this is heaven
then, before it all got complicated;
wet and warm and neither longed for
nor rejected, with John and Paul
in another room singing 'Love Me Do'.

Lydia Macpherson

nothing

the waffle iron
of the queen mary
makes unsymmetric wedges.

fanatics know
how many pounds of spaghetti
in the bucket
john lennon forks to the fat woman
in Magical Mystery Tour
but they can't prove it.

[one minute pause]

online profile check-boxes
and room for narrative
to help you choose me.

that a big noodle?
she asks.
fair question.

[one minute pause]

"You wanna try some
it's got a very nice flavour
but a little bit on the greasy side?"

[one minute pause]

the teenage boy fingers
his father's change, bills and coins.
abstractions
        pain teenagers to their growing bones.

dad let's him calculate a tip
pocket the rest

he blows a straw wrapper
at his father's face
then places it on his arm,
then strokes his ear and cheek with it.

Craig Cotter

PARENTS' EVENING

We feel she may be cheating
at reading and spelling.
She has failed to grasp the planets
and the laws of science,
has proven violent in games
and fakes asthma for attention.

She is showing promise with the Odyssey,
has learned to darn starfish
and knitted a patch for the scarecrow.
She seems to enjoy measuring rain,
pretending her father is a Beatle
and insists upon your death
as the conclusion to all her stories.

Rhian Edwards

SKINNY

The day Paterson held magnesium
in the Bunsen without tongs
and got himself whisked to hospital
with second degree burns
eight years before they invented
Flammozene in the Falklands

was the day I knew one day I'd die,
my faith in God less tested
than my love of *The White Album* he'd lent me,
'Revolution 9' spinning round my head
as I turned to see him stretching
to ignite the starburst of flame.

Anthony Wilson

JOHN LENNON'S ROLLS ROYCE

I wait for Maureen in the hall
of the Flora Dugdale Home for laughing girls,
girls who take it in turns to peer round the door
at the boy in the stifling yellow polo-neck.

Blood-cheeked, we turn the corner
before we hold hands, catch our breath, speak.
I take her to see John Lennon's
psychedelic Rolls Royce. It rains.

It rains so hard we are soaked
and she slips on the muddy verge.

In the bus shelter: Maureen's tartan skirt
stuck to her legs, me fiddling with its silver safety-pin,

the lurch for a kiss, the taste
of Trebor mints, rain.

Martin Figura

CLOUD NINE

for St Silas School and Liverpool Community Spirit

There's a sign saying Cloud Nine
in the boarded-up shop next to The Empress
near where Ringo lived, but nine
was always John's number –
Newcastle Road – Revolution – Dream – Imagine
a community where dreams are replaced
by decisions with the word
'Demolish' written all over this part
of Liverpool Eight because they say so

and they think so in St Silas School today –
nine-years-old Yusef on rhythm guitar
in assembly – but that was always John's number
as rain drums on the windows
of where Ringo went and 'Rain'
was his best drumming ever
but John's song – listen:
along Wynnstay, Voelas and Rhiwlas streets,
listen in Gwydir, Elwy, Teilo, Dovey

where a cloud saying Number Nine
looks over the rooftops of what's left
of shops near the Empress,
as red berries cling to fresh leaves,
the Cathedral staring down the length of Windsor Street,
as a smart car cruises the neighbourhood
and pigeons in Admiral Grove,
unaware of sentimental journeys,
get their heads down to drink in the autumn rain.

Phil Bowen

PENNY LANE, ILLINOIS

No bankers, firemen, or barbers figured in this Midwestern teenager's microcosm, yet I sang of them again and again, of suburbia with its routines and oddities, a place at once foreign and familiar. What was a mac, or, more worryingly, fish and finger pies? I was corn husk and thrift shop, purple jeans and prairie, but Penny Lane lay just around the corner every time I sang.

Carrie Etter

FORBIDDEN FRUITS

sometime around Brezhnev's sixth Order of Lenin
Hank was in Moscow on business,
where, as a special treat
(after the compulsory collective farm
and the equally compulsory Bolshoi),
he got taken to a Party-only night club

>   *Dean Tempest, International Vocalist,*
>   *Greatest English Act since the Beatles*

Dean was a redundant miner from Barnsley
with an unusually imaginative agent
who did a fair Tom Jones impersonation
to accordion and balalaika accompaniment

Dean reckoned Russia was a right good laugh

just tell them everything's by the Beatles,
pal, you can't go wrong

what happens if they check?

you ever tried buying a Beatles record here?

under socialism, comrade, we have
full employment
        no crises of overproduction

Gordon Wardman

EXPATRIATES

Here in Iran we're just
'the Amreekans', 'the Brits'.
We move conspicuously

through streets sounding
with the clatter of strange words
(it's always the same,

this journey each traveler makes
to become a stranger) yet
still we insist on carrying

a land along with us
on our tongues. Old
hippies, untethered by speech,

hitch on down to Hiraz,
up to Rasht, looking
for hash and poets' graves

and it's they who should be
our prophets in this land,
they who can live on mere

gestures and mute wanderlust.
But the rest of us, trenched
together in this great

bazaar, come to crave
the Hollywood dialogue,
the soft wrinkle of paperbacks

loaned from hand to hand,
the exhilarating rush
of *thump-thump-pahhh*

in rock lyrics. We hide
inside our English, scratch
about for Beatles tapes,

and say without thinking,
"OK, it's OK",
insistent in a way

the Persians made fun of,
imitating our strange
and urgent sounds, but

damn it! yes, we're different
and we stake fervent claims
to our sleazy novels,

our Corn Flakes boxes,
or Maltese Falcon,
our Sgt. Pepper's,

to what we groan in bed
together, to "oh yeahhh"
what words make real

even here where
we've got nothing to say
but "it's OK".

Shelli Jankowski-Smith

LOVE

After Parfitt and Rossi had softened us up
and, past reasoning, something stirred at the sight
of the packed stadium – some surge of hope
for the power of change – and hours before Freddie Mercury
had us eating out of his hand with 'Bohemian Rhapsody'
and just a blur by the time Geldof lost it on air, stoving,
"give us your money, just give us the fucking money" –
there was Elvis Costello alone downstage saying he'd need
a little help with "this old northern English folk song".
And we were nonplussed before the first chords but when
he got to "Nothing that you can do that can't be done..." tears were
being snuffled back in a gut-lurch of ownership: this thing's ours,
and it's up there with Auden and his "love one another or die",
and bigger than Larkin's "what will survive of us" – and maybe
this *was* all we'd need – 'love', for god sake – deep in an age
of Bananarama, barrowboys and bankers, Thatcher
and Reagan – and here it comes again, its meeting of East
and West, its mantra, its harmonies as hand-me downs
for my teenage daughters who know it, "yes, dad, of course
we do, you mean the 'lovelovelove one' ", and they're away
with some imaginary brass ("Da-da-dada-da...")
before filling the house with their singalong, making the dogs
go doolally with their new take on some old English folk song.

Peter Carpenter

EXCHANGE VALUES

"Money is not only the medium of exchange, but also a store of value,
and the standard in terms of which... all kinds of relations between men
are more or less rigidly fixed."
Piero Sraffa

1

Piero Sraffa, I remember,
came up to me once in Barclay's Bank.
"Young man," he said, "is that today's date"
– gesturing toward the blurred blank
of a wall – "or the Interest Rate?"
I said: "It's the thirteenth of September".

2

But what could I say to those wealthy Japanese
tourists traipsing by my parents' house
off to photograph Paul McCartney's?
'Hello! Goodbye!' of course –
like the school kids do when I'm there
as they pass in their limousine bus,
wave, turn giggling heads to stare
at an alien, forgivably curious.

Peter Robinson

THE LAST PANDA

Unprecedented economic growth in my native country
has brought mochaccino and broadband to where there
was nothing but misery and disease, yet with loss of
habitat the inevitable consequence; even the glade I was
born in is now a thirty-storey apartment block with valet
parking and a nail salon. They scrape DNA from the
inside of my cheek and freeze it, 'just in case'. To the
world I'm known by my stage name and am Richard to
family and friends, but never Dick. Well-meaning
tourists visiting the Cavern throw pastries and pieces of
fruit despite notices regarding my sensitive nature and
strict diet. I cried all night when John was shot, rubbed
the tired circles of my eyes till they turned black. Please
do not tap on the glass. The sixties did it for everyone, I
mean EVERYONE, and what people failed to grasp
about Chairman Mao was that despite the drab-looking
suits and systematic violations of basic human rights
he liked a good tune as much as the next man.
Liverpool's a great shag but you wouldn't want to marry
it. They named a potato snack in my honour and also a
small family cat, how many people can say that? Fans
write to me from as far away as Papua New Guinea and I
insist on responding personally. In fact my 'sixth digit' –
an enlarged wrist bone which functions as a thumb –
means that handwriting comes easier to me than it does to
many other creatures, for example the Rolling Stones. If
I didn't believe there was one more hit record in me I
swear I'd end it now. In the dream, there's still a Paul
and a George somewhere in the high valleys of Ganzu
Province, classic period white shirts and black ties, mop
tops down to their shoulders, strumming away. These
sunglasses have prescription lenses and are not just for
effect. Reviewing my Wikipedia entry I note that
'Yellow Submarine' and 'Octopus's Garden' anticipated
the absurdist trend in rock'n'roll by at least a decade.
Every first Tuesday in the month the lady vet gives me a
hand job but due to the strength of the tranquilliser the

pleasure is all hers. Years ago they brought Yoko to the
doors of my cage but it wouldn't have worked; I let the
slow snowball of my head roll sadly eastwards and
stared towards the Himalayas. In the whole cosmos
there's only me. What hurts most isn't the loneliness
but the withering disrespect: as if they'd dropped a couple
of bamboo sticks into my paws and I'd just played along.

Simon Armitage

CLASS ACT

"bumped into history today,
a million punters down the Cavern Club,
             you couldn't get them all inside,
                     there'd be no place to hide,
seems that almost all the so-called regulars
                             had lied,

so much for turning on…"

the line's gone dead –
a flickering black-and-white
of screaming girls and good old Harold
and George bemusedly young –
nothing so unusual as the recently past

but it was a time they still had lines
and Hank's was crossed on the Fab Four
– OK, more proletarian than Cliff,
NOT AMERICAN like white trash Elvis,
into Peace, and jokes at the Royals' expense,
you could almost give them five for that
but what about the MBEs?
the Maharishi, Yoko Ono,
the fucking vegetarianism?
the sixties made it hard to grade our heroes
and the line broke around the Beatles;
with them the classless society went nuclear,
the Beatles were a commisar's hell,
and Hank's testimony stands mute of malice

– what do you really think about them, Tam?

– I remember that *Sergeant Pepper*
  fucking art college crap;
  I preferred the Rolling Stones,
  you knew where you were with them boys –
  pissing up against a wall.

Gordon Wardman

102

BACK IN THE USSR

for Fergus

I was born in Ireland too late
for Beatlemania. Yet they opened a door
in our town and the small desires of the Fifties –
formica kitchens, labour saving appliances –
went out while less easy ones stepped in. Freedom
was the word we used for this but never understood.
The big girl next door said the Beatles were the thing
and so they were. We learned the words and sung
the tunes like anthems of a revolution
against domestic obedience, an expectant Church.
We talked excitedly of Hare Krishna and LSD, and although
a long way from the daily pain of Vietnam, we wanted
Peace to have its chance. It was a sort of education.
I stacked shelves in Dunne's Stores to buy Sergeant Pepper
clothes. My elder brother listened to them
on his new transistor radio, the same one
on which he heard, he said, real-time
Radio Free Prague crashed into silence. He said
he heard the jackboots on the stairs, the studio door
bashed in. He became a local celebrity of sorts,
an authority on East European politics, for a while.
But everything goes back to those who fuck
the rest, those with wealth and power or who
have stepped up to the plate and grabbed a handful.
Yet these words of Freedom, Love and Peace
are like a fever. The virus lives on, there's been
an unexpected outbreak in the Arab Spring.
I listen to my son who's strumming 'Back in the USSR'
on his guitar, as if there's no redemption in the past,
as if everything that's won is somehow lost.

Frank Dullaghan

shaw street

it tested our repertoire
and patience
that residency at the red
star social club

every time I picked
up the mandolin
someone wanted advice
on tuning his balalaika
and the drunk always woke
at some point to shout
comrades do you
know guantanamera

when we'd already
established all we knew
was the two word refrain
and the creepy spoken bit
from the sandpipers'
version that went
the words mean
I am a truthful man
from the land of
the palm trees

but we weren't unkind
we gave him a quick chorus
then lulled him back to sleep
with some flaming verses
from working class hero

now that
was something to be

Alasdair Paterson

THANK U VERY MUCH

Taking a break from recording at Olympic Studios
the Gallaghers, large as life, were outside my local
that August evening, when, pen and notebook in hand
I strolled past as inconspicuously as possible.

But in vain. It was Noel who recognised me
and well-nigh dragged me over to their table.
Liam bought the round: red wine for his brother,
large whiskey for himself, and a lager top for me.

"Tell us about John Lennon." "Tell us about the Sixties."
"Tell us about…" A double-act that was difficult
to penetrate. "Relax, lads," I said, "well understand
your excitement, but one at a time, please."

"Tell us about Scaffold." "Tell us about Brian Epstein."
"Calm down, calm down," I said with Aintree irony.
"If you're really interested, why not hit my web-site?"
Liam removed his shades.   "Gob-shite."

Roger McGough

the grapes

the sozzled singalong years
ah there were giants
on the earth those days
and they had their seasons
like the famous albie
widger in apple-blossom time

the fireplace was notoriously
haunted and someone in the grate
somewhere heard every word
while the continents drifted
audibly as you sang
see the pyrenees along the nile

then it was our moment
the young ones who were
loosening the sky with diamonds
to a burglar sound of broken
glass till there was light

I remember it well
that translucence
the beautiful liquids
it was the dawning
of the age of aquariums

Alasdair Paterson

SPLICE

Cocaine, methedrine, heroin,
percodan. Fat Elvis,
dead. Sam Cooke mysteriously dead. Joplin
drunk and dead. Lennon.
Hendrix. Morrison, Cobain. Whatever
the price, they were willing to pay. Yeah,
yeah but I say rock and roll
is a church meeting, a gathering
around tribal drums. Boys
and girls sing to mothers and fathers.
Gods sleep like kittens
in the hollows of guitars.
The Beatles reunite
and here's the proof: in 'Real Love', McCartney
wraps his voice around the voice of his dead
partner. Don't we all wish for one more chance
to get it right, lights shining on a photograph
of four new leather jackets or the snapshot
where the circle around a Formica kitchen table,
Scrabble game in progress.
behind our seven letters we wonder
how to connect one word to another.

E.J. Miller Laino

DESERT NIGHTS

For George Harrison, 1943-2001.

PBS Reno
just played
the Concert for George.
Stepping outdoors,
the moon is bright,
an incandescent ball,
glowing.

Weatherman said
"partly cloudy".
A sprinkle of stars twinkle
in the Northern sky.
The night is brisk;
the crunch of ice beneath my feet,
recalls a bundled up childhood
of sledding
down snow white hillocks
in a small Eastern town,
so far away in time and memory.
A gentle wind is blowing,

though most of the land
is now brown earth,
not snow.
It is the sounds one remembers
long after the visuals are gone.
Or going.

To see the night sky
in all its glory,
and to hear George Harrison's music
lilt across this high desert plain,
is breathtaking.
And to know glaciers were right here
long ago.

This was the very edge of them,
for a while.
A strong connection is growing.

Sitar strings sing
and reverberate
in this desert night,
his music still flowing.

Sharmagne Leland-St. John

RELIC

One of John Lennon's teeth is expected to make £10,000
when it is auctioned next month.
BBC News, 19th October 2011

In the kitchen, bracing
his pain between the table
and the stove, he tore
the tooth from the gum

with a wet crunch, gave it,
bloody, as a souvenir,
and walked out beyond
decay.

After fifty years it looks
like forgotten popcorn
or a knot of Wrigley's
chewed past stretch.

Only the root suggests
it was once nerved-in
to a jaw that tenderised
Lennon's meat.

What will you do with it?

Keep it in a matchbox
in a jam jar in a football sock
underneath the bed, warmed
each night knowing it's there.

Ask your stunned dentist
to replace the molar so you
can share that grin
with the bathroom mirror.

Plant it behind the shed,
marked by bamboo,
and watch for bone
to break the soil.

Or, on days your own tune
won't play, put it in your ear
like a shell, and hear
the long dead croon:

"love, love me do".

Katherine Stansfield

CRADLE SONG

Golden slumbers kiss your eyes,
Smiles awake you when you rise;
Sleep, pretty wantons, do not cry,
And I will sing a lullaby,
Rock them, rock them, lullaby.

Care is heavy, therefore sleep you,
You are care, and care must keep you;
Sleep, pretty wantons, do not cry,
And I will sing a lullaby,
Rock them, rock them, lullaby.

Thomas Dekker

ACKNOWLEDGEMENTS

Simon Armitage: 'The Last Panda' is from *Seeing Stars* (2010), © and is reproduced here by permission or the author and Faber and Faber.

Kimmy Beach's poems are from *Fake Paul* (Turnstone Press, 2005).

Pam Bernard's poem is from her collection *Across the Dark* (Main Street Rag Press, 2002.

Phil Bowen's poems are reproduced by permission of the author. 'Thirteen in Sixty Three' appeared in *Things We Said Today* (Stride, 1995).

Paul Butler's poem is reproduced by permission of the author. It first appeared in *Things We Said Today* (Stride, 1995).

John Canfield's poem is reproduced by permission of the author.

Peter Carpenter's poem is reproduced by permission of the author.

Suzanne Conway's poem is reproduced by permission of the author.

Craig Cotter's poem is reproduced by permission of the author.

Mike Cunningham's poem is reproduced by permission of the author. It first appeared in *Things We Said Today* (Stride, 1995).

Brian Daldorph's poem is reproduced by permission of the author.

Andy Darlington's poem is reproduced by permission of the author. It first appeared in *Things We Said Today* (Stride, 1995).

Tim Dooley's poem is collected in *Keeping Time* (Salt, 2008).

Carol Ann Duffy's poems are to be found in her *Selected Poems* (Penguin, 2006) and are reproduced with the permission of the author and Rogers Coleridge and White.

Frank Dullaghan's poem is reproduced by permission of the author.

Jane Draycott's poem is reproduced by permission of the author.

Rhian Edwards's poem is from *Clueless Dogs* (Seren, 2012).

Carrie Etter's poem is reproduced by permission of the author.

Paul Farley's '11th February 1963' was published in *The Ice Age* (Picador, 2002) and is reprinted by kind permission of the author and Picador.

Elaine Feinstein's poem 'For the Beatles' is published in her *Collected Poems & Translations* (Carcanet).

Mike Ferguson's poem is reproduced by permission of the author. It first appeared in *Things We Said Today* (Stride, 1995).

Martin Figura's poem is reproduced by permission of the author.

Peter Finch's poem is reproduced by permission of the author.

Damian Furniss's poems are reproduced by permission of the author.

Allen Ginsberg: 'First Party at Ken Kesey's with Hell's Angels' was published in *Holy Soul Jelly Roll* (Rhino Entertainment, 1998).

Ann Gray's poem is reproduced by permission of the author.

Paul Groves's poem is from *Wowsers* (Seren, 2002).

Geoff Hattersley's poem is reproduced by permission of the author. It first appeared in *Things We Said Today* (Stride, 1995).

Adrian Henri: 'New York City Blues' is from *Penny Arcade* and is reproduced by permission of Jonathan Cape Ltd.

William Heyen: 'The Colony' was first published as a privately printed postcard in 1988.

Andy Jackson's poem is reproduced by permission of the author.

Pamela Johnson's poem is reproduced by permission of the author. It first appeared in *Things We Said Today* (Stride, 1995).

Shelli Jankowski-Smith

Kenny Knight's poem is reproduced by permission of the author. It first appeared in *Things We Said Today* (Stride, 1995).

Peter Lane's poem is reproduced by permission of the author. It first appeared in *Things We Said Today* (Stride, 1995).

Philip Larkin: 'Annus Mirabilis' is from *High Windows*, © the Estate of Philip Larkin and reprinted by permission of Faber & Faber Ltd.

Sharmagne Leland-St.John's poem was first published in *Silver Tears and Time* (Quill and Parchment Press).

Lizzy Lister's poem is reproduced by permission of the author. It first appeared in *Things We Said Today* (Stride, 1995).

Rupert Loydell's 'The White Poem' is © the author, and printed by his permission.

Lachlan Mackinnon: 'On the Roof of the World' is from *The Jupiter Collisions*, © Lachlan Mackinnon and reprinted by permission of Faber & Faber Ltd.

Lydia Macpherson's poem was first published in *Smiths Knoll* and is reproduced by permission of the author.

Roger McGough: 'Conversation on a Train' was first publsihed in *The Glass Room* (Jonathan Cape) and is reproduced by permission of Peters, Fraser & Dunlop. 'Thank U Very Much' is also reproduced by permission of Peters, Fraser & Dunlop.

E.J Miller Laino: 'Splice' first appeared in *In My Life: Encounters with the Beatles* (1998)

Kim Moore's poem is reproduced by permission of the author.

Alasdair Paterson's poems are reproduced by permission of the author.

Estill Pollock's poem is reproduced by permission of the author.

Sheenagh Pugh's poem is from *The Beautiful Lie* (Seren, 2002).

Jeremy Reed's poems are reprinted by kind permission of the author.

Peter Robinson's 'There Are Avenues' is taken from the book of that name, published by Brodie Press in 2006.

Carol Rumens's poem appears in *The Yellow Nib* magazine.

Maurice Rutherford's poem is reproduced by permission of the author.

Katherine Stansfield's poem was first published on the *Cadaverine* website and is reproduced by permission of the author.

Amy Wack's poem is reproduced by permission of the author.

Gordon Wardman's poems are reproduced by permission of the author. They first appeared in *Things We Said Today* (Stride, 1995).

Nerys Williams's poem is reproduced by permission of the author.

Anthony Wilson's poem is reproduced by permission of the author.

David Wojahn's poems are from *Mystery Train* (University of Pittsburgh Press, 1990).

David Woolley's poem is reproduced by permission of the author.

Glyn Wright's poem is reproduced by permission of the author. It first appeared in *Things We Said Today* (Stride, 1995).

Tamar Yoseloff's poem was first published in *Sweetheart* (Slow Dancer Press, 1998).

Every effort has been made to contact the rights holders of these poems. We will be pleased to rectify any omissions in future editions.

CONTRIBUTORS' NOTES

Simon Armitage is a freelance writer, broadcaster and playwright who has written extensively for radio and television. He was made CBE in 2010, and awarded the Hay Medal for Poetry in 2012. His latest collections are *The Death of King Arthur* (Faber) and *Black Roses* (Pomona), both 2012.

Kimmy Beach's fifth book is *The Last Temptation of Bond* (University of Alberta Press, 2013). A Beatles fan since the age of nine, her favourite song is and always has been 'Lovely Rita', except for when it's 'Why Don't We Do It in the Road?'.Kimmy lives in Alberta, Canada.

Pam Bernard is the prize-winning author of three collections of poetry, most recently *Blood Garden: An Elegy for Raymond*. She is a professor at the New Hampshire Institute of Art.

Nathaniel Blue visited London in early 1967 in between stints living in New York and Los Angeles and attended The Million Dollar Light and Sound Rave at the Roundhouse on 28 January where he was among the few to hear Carnival of Light. He is now a Pentecostal missionary in Peru.

Phil Bowen first saw the Beatles in the window of the photographer Albert Marrion's shop in Penny Lane towards the end of 1962. Favourite track is 'I'll Be Back'.

Paul Butler: "I have a copy of the original sheet music for 'Love Me Do' which somebody gave me way back when. I expect few people bought it at the time as even a novice guitarist could figure out the three chords. Three chords.Three words. And aged twelve the first pop song I had ever heard that would not leave my head."

John Canfield grew up in Cornwall and now lives and writes in London. He trained as an actor and has performed in the West End and on BBC Radio. He has been published most recently in *Oxford Poetry* and in Sidekick Books' forthcoming anthology *Coin Opera II*.

Peter Carpenter remembers the singles his sister bought in the sixties – he loved the B sides, especially 'Rain' with its backwards lyrics at the end. His favourite album is *Revolver* and his most recent collection, *Just Like That – New & Selected Poems* was published by Smith Doorstop in 2012.

Suzanne Conway is a teacher who has poems in most of the leading magazines including *Poetry Review, The North, The Rialto, Smiths Knoll, Ambit, Magma, The London Magazine* and *Seam*. She is working on a PhD in Creative and Critical Writing with Glyn Maxwell. Favourite songs: 'No Reply' and 'Baby It's You'.

Craig Cotter: "In 1978 I was writing an undergraduate paper on The Beatles at Michigan State University. I decided to call John Lennon at the

Dakota for his take. When the operator answered I said, "Can you put me through to John Lennon?" Operator: "You want to speak to John Lennon?" Craig: "Yes." Operator: "OK, I'll put you right through. [Pause as my heart jumped. Then, with kindness and some sarcasm]: I can't do that." He gave me the address of the Dakota, and I sent Lennon a letter."

Mike Cunningham went to St. Edward's in Liverpool. Four members of his class took on the names of the Beatles. This meant that someone whose real name was Paul became George, and someone else Paul. Ringo's real name was Peter Stamper who was also known as Frog. Surprisingly there was no-one in the class actually called Ringo.

Brian Daldorph was born in Harrogate, Yorkshire. He teaches at the University of Kansas and Douglas County Jail. He edits *Coal City Review*. His most recent book of poetry is *Jail Time* (Original Plus Press, 2009).

Andy Darlington is a Yorkshire based poet and music journalist. He writes for Videovista website, and writes about Folk and Roots for *R2: Rock 'n' Reel* magazine.

Thomas Dekker (1572-1632) was a dramatist and pamphleteer whose work was typically bold and provocative, making his ballad, 'Cradle Song' a departure.

Tim Dooley's poems are collected in *Keeping Time* (2008) and *Imagined Rooms* (2010), both published by Salt. He is reviews editor of *Poetry London*, a tutor for the Poetry School, and an Arts Mentor for the Koestler Trust. His experience of The Beatles is one of continual rediscovery. Yes, it is.

Carol Ann Duffy was born in Glasgow and read philosophy at Liverpool University. She is a poet and playwright, and writes for both adults and children. She is OBE and CBE, Fellow of the Royal Society of Literature, and the Poet Laureate. Her latest publication is *The Bees* (2011).

Frank Dullaghan is an Irish poet living in Dubai. He began his teenage years in the wake of Beatlemania and was old enough to be shocked and saddened when they split up. The imagery in Eleanor Rigby ("face that she kept in a jar by the door") still holds poetic power for him.

Jane Draycott's most recent collection is *Over* (Carcanet, 2009). Her translation of the medieval dream-vision *Pearl* was published by Carcanet in 2011. Her favourite Beatles albums are *Sgt Pepper* and *Abbey Road*.

Rhian Edwards' first full collection of poems, *Clueless Dogs*, was published by Seren in 2012, and was shortlisted for the Forward Prize for First Collection. She won the John Tripp Award for Spoken Poetry 2011/12.

Carrie Etter is originally from Illinois. She moved to Southern California, and to London in 2001. Her latest collection is *Divining for Starters*

(Shearsman), 2011. She is an Associate Lecturer at Bath Spa University.

Paul Farley was born in Liverpool. He writes widely for radio and on art and literature. He is Professor of Poetry at Lancaster University. His latest collection, *The Dark Film*, was shortlisted for the 2012 T.S. Eliot Prize.

Elaine Feinstein MA., FRSL, DLitt, is a prize-winning poet, novelist and biographer. She was born in the same city as the Beatles, read English at Cambridge, and lived there for quarter of a century. She has travelled across the globe to read her poems. Now in London, she has just finished writing her memoirs. Her most recent book of poems is *Cities*, (Carcanet 2010).

Mike Ferguson: "Iowa 1964, my father wouldn't allow me a Beatles haircut. It wasn't until moving to England in 1967 that my Brylcreem quiff was permitted to a fringe, but that's only because the Beach Boys had grown their hair too! Favourite Beatles songs: Strawberry Fields Forever and Lady Madonna."

Martin Figura was born in the same hospital as John Lennon – this is not widely known. His very first memories from life have a Beatles sound-track. He queued around the block on Saturdays for the movies. 'Yellow Submarine' got him dancing in front of the telly.

Peter Finch was born in Cardiff, where he still lives. The fat girl from the next street introduced him to 'Please Please Me' by inviting him round to hear it when her parents were out. "This is the real stuff," she told him. He's never been the same since.

Damian Furniss destroyed his mother's collection of Beatles singles while still at playschool. He still remembers how good the beach stripe sleeves and red labels of their early releases looked when coloured in, and claims to have invented scratching several years before Grand Wizard Theodore.

Allen Ginsberg was born in Newark, New Jersey in 1926. He was one of the major figures of the world-changing Beat Generation in the 1950s, publishing the seminal *Howl* in 1956. John and George attended his 39th birthday party in London. He died in 1997.

Ann Gray: "I was with my sister, standing in our bedroom, looking out at another dreary day, when I first heard 'Love Me Do' and it made my heart beat faster. I saw them, the next year, at the Regal. I chose George. You name any track, I hear it in my head, impossible to have a favourite."

Paul Groves: "The Beatles were the backdrop to my youth. I first encoun-tered them in *The New Musical Express* in 1962. Favourite track? 'Another Girl' for its blitheness. Most polished single? 'Lady Madonna'. My wedding reception was at The Angel Hotel, Abergavenny in 1972 where the Fab Four overnighted following their knock-out concert at the town ten years earlier.

Geoff Hattersley lives in Barnsley, one of the Yorkshire towns Paul visited with his sheepdog, Martha.

Adrian Henri was born in Liverpool in 1932, and was a poet and painter. He was part of the 'Mersey Sound' with Roger McGough and Brian Patten, which ran alongside the Beatles in the 1960s in establishing a voice for popular culture for the youth of Britain. He made albums with the poetry band The Liverpool Scene and published his *Collected Poems 1967-85* in 1986 (Bloodaxe). He died in December 2000, the day after receiving the freedom of the city of Liverpool.

William Heyen lives in Brockport, NY. His recent books of poetry include *Shoah Train* (a National Book Award finalist), *A Poetics of Hiroshima* (a Chautauqua Literary & Scientific Circle selection), *The Football CoTrporations*, and *Straight's Suite for Craig Cotter & Frank O'Hara*. Sometimes he thinks he has devoted his life to family & poetry to try to answer the question: "all the lonely people/where do they all come from?" He's grateful that in 1988 after Yoko Ono saw 'The Colony' she sent him a card signed "Love".

Andy Jackson (b. Salford 1965) has appeared in *Magma, Gutter* and other magazines. Debut collection *The Assassination Museum* (Red Squirrel Press) appeared in 2010, and he is editor of *Split Screen*, an anthology of poems inspired by TV & film (2012). "My Beatles go-to album is *Rubber Soul* – 14 minor miracles from a band about to become a legend".

Pamela Johnson has published novels – *Under Construction* and *Deep Blue Silence* – and poems in anthologies and magazines. She teaches creative writing on the MA at Goldsmiths' and runs the literary website, Words Unlimited, http://wordsunlimited.typepad.com/words_unlimited/ June 1967, glued to the TV for the first ever live global broadcast, including 'All You Need Is Love' sung in Abbey Road Studios. Epic.

Shelli Jankowski-Smith lives in Massachusetts, where she teaches Reiki and other wellbeing techniques. She is co-editor of *In My Life: Encounters with the Beatles*.

Kenny Knight lives in Devonport. His collection *The Honicknowle Book of the Dead* (Shearsman) appeared in 2009.

Peter Lane was born in Stoke-on-Trent. His collection *Small Times in a Big Office* was published by Smith Doorstop.

Philip Larkin was born in Coventry in 1922. He was a poet and novelist, and the most influential poet of his generation, coming to prominence with *The Less Deceived*, in 1955. He continued to work as a Senior Librarian, and was also jazz critic for *The Daily Telegraph*. He declined the position of Poet Laureate in 1984, and died the following year.

Sharmagne Leland-St.John: "I was a guest every night during their stay in Los Angeles on their first LA tour. The first words I ever heard George utter were: "Who's got the peanut butter"? Later I was at music school with George, studying Indian music. The first song I learned to play as a raga was 'This Bird Has Flown (Norwegian Wood)'. My partner and I played the music behind Dr. Timothy Leary's Slide Show Celebrations. We always opened with this song. The Beatles and their music was a way of life for us. It helped us to get our foot in the door as performers. Their music will live forever, especially in my heart.

Lizzy Lister's first record purchases were the red and blue albums, *Rock and Roll vols. One and Two*. Graduated to *Rarities* on a teak radiogram, squeaking through a coverless *Beatles Complete* on a Honher recorder until 1981 when *Vital Vinyl* replaced *Revolver* and 'Eleanor Rigby' fell to Generation X's 'Ready Steady Go'.

Rupert Loydell lives in Cornwall with his family and far too many books, CDs and LPs including a picture disc of Paul McCartney's 'The Frog Song'. He is Senior Lecturer in Creative Writing at University College Falmouth, his most recent collection of poetry, *Wildlife* (Shearsman).

Lachlan Mackinnon was born in Scotland in 1956. He is a poet, critic and journalist. He was at school in Detroit when the Beatles appeared on bubble-gum cards. He had never heard of them, but they added to the kudos of being British. His most recent collection is *Small Hours* (Faber).

Lydia Macpherson's poems have been widely published in magazines and anthologies and she has been placed in major competitions. She has an MA in Creative Writing from Royal Holloway University of London. and was nominated for the inaugural Faber New Poets scheme. Her favourite Beatles track is 'Ticket to Ride'.

Roger McGough was born in Liverpool in 1937. He is a poet, broadcaster, children's author and playwright. Sharing the 'Mersey Sound' with Henri and Patten, he also had a musical career alongside Paul's brother, Mike McGear in The Scaffold, and then in Grimms, an anarchic merger of Scaffold, Henri's Liverpool Scene and The Bonzo Dog Doodah Band. His latest collection is *As Far as I Know* (Penguin, 2012).

E.J Miller Laino lives and teaches in Florida. Her collection *Girl Hurt* appeared from Alice James Books, and she is co-editor of *In My Life: Encounters with the Beatles*.

Kim Moore's first pamphlet *If We Could Speak Like Wolves* was published in May 2012. In 2010 she won an Eric Gregory Award and the Geoffrey Dearmer prize. "Whenever I hear a Beatles song, it reminds me of Sunday evenings, when we were allowed to pick records to play from my mum's record collection. We always picked a Beatles song, whilst my dad sulked because we didn't choose any of his music."

Alasdair Paterson lived in Liverpool in the 70s and 80s and played in a band full of survivors from the Merseybeat era. He'd always been a Beatles fan, but the experience of being there very much deepened appreciation of the songs. Favourite track: 'A Day in the Life'.

Estill Pollock's publications include the book cycles *Blackwater Quartet* and *Relic Environments Trilogy*. Visit www.estillpollock-poetry.com.

Sheenagh Pugh was born in 1950, so her adolescence coincided with Beatlemania. Her most enduring memory is of the LP *Help!* coming out, and everyone in the school yard arguing about whether 'You've Got To Hide Your Love Away' was really a disguised gay love song.

Jeremy Reed is a Jersey-born writer and poet. He has published 50 major works in 25 years. His wide range of inspirations include many pop music figures including Elvis, Lou Reed, Scott Walker and Marc Almond. His latest collection is *Piccadilly Bongo* (2010).

Peter Robinson is Professor of English and American Literature at the University of Reading. His most recent collection of poetry is *The Returning Sky* (2012, Shearsman Books). He grew up mainly in Liverpool while the Beatles were releasing such songs as 'Penny Lane' and 'Strawberry Fields'. They were thus responsible for his first realizing that art could be made from your immediate surroundings. His mother lives round the corner from the McCartney house in Forthlin Road.

For **Carol Rumens**, the Beatles' songs were an essential sound-track of the 'very heaven' of the early sixties. She had the Croydon version of the Vidal Sassoon haircut, dropped out of university and sang 'All You Need is Love' believing it to be true. That was then. Her most recent collection is *De Chirico's Threads* (Seren, 2010).

Now in his nineties, **Maurice Rutherford**'s favourite Beatles song is 'She's Leaving Home'. He also admires Lennon's 'Imagine'. He has published two recent collections with Shoestring Press: *And Saturday is Christmas* (2011) and *Flip to Philip Larkin* (2012).

Katherine Stansfield teaches creative writing at Aberystwyth University. Her first collection of poems, *Playing House*, will be published by Seren in 2014. Her first novel, *The Visitor*, will be published by Parthian in 2013. Her favourite song by The Beatles is 'And Your Bird Can Sing'.

Amy Wack was born in Florida, raised in San Diego, California, and completed an MFA in writing from Columbia University in New York City. She currently lives in Cardiff, Wales where she works as poetry editor for Seren. Her poems and reviews have appeared in magazines in the UK and USA.

Gordon Wardman was born in 1948. He has published two novels, and several collections of poetry, often featuring his alter-ego Hank Gilbey.

He lives in Harlow, Essex.

Nerys Williams, originally from West Wales, published her first collection of poetry *Sound Archive* (2011) with Seren. The winner of the Strong First Volume Prize, she also lectures at University College Dublin. Nerys wishes she could have witnessed the recording of 'A Day in the Life'.

Anthony Wilson is the author of *Riddance* (Worple Press, 2012) and *Love for Now* (Impress Books, 2012). His love affair with the Beatles began when he was given *Revolver* for his tenth birthday.

David Wojahn teaches poetry at Vermont College of Fine Arts and Virginia Commonwealth University. He often takes on subjects of significance in popular culture, not least in *Mystery Train* (University of Piuttsburgh Press, 1990). He has won the Pushcart Prize three times and has been shortlisted for the Pulitzer.

David Woolley first remembers hearing the newly released 'She Loves You' coming from his older sister's bedroom. Ten years on he bought a copy from a friend at school, but lost the replacement 'hole' in the middle of the 45 on the way home.

Glyn Wright: "The first I hear is. Nineteen sixty two. School holidays. Mather Avenue. Blomfield one way, Forthlin the other. A bunch of kids on the verge. A girl's voice, 'There's this band. Lads from around here. Someone says they're gonna make a record...' And the rest in lost in the gabble."

Tamar Yoseloff's most recent collections are *The City with Horns* (Salt, 2011) and *Formerly*, with photographs by Vici MacDonald (Hercules Editions, 2012). She is also the author of two collaborative editions with the artist Linda Karshan and the editor of *A Room to Live In: A Kettle's Yard Anthology*. Her favourite Beatle is George.

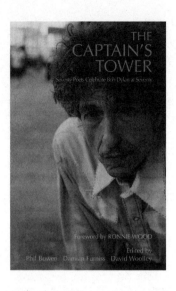

The Captain's Tower

Edited by Phil Bowen, Damian Furniss and David Woolley

Foreword by Ronnie Wood

Published to celebrate Bob Dylan's 70th Birthday, *The Captain's Tower* is an anthology of poems concerned with Dylan's life, his work, and his cultural impact. One of the most distinguished lyricists of the post-war period, Dylan has entertained and inspired poets, writers generally, and millions of ordinary fans with the imagery, wit and technique of his writing, be it in songs of love, protest, faith or pure Dylan-ness.

In this book the poets respond to Dylan's creativity, capacity to inspire and his enormous influence on culture and writing. Here are poems by Allen Ginsberg, Lachlan Mackinnon, Glyn Maxwell, Matthew Sweeney, Jeremy Reed, Linda Chase, Linda France, Mark Ford, Roger McGough, Roddy Lumsden, Paul Muldoon, Simon Armitage, Caroline Bird, Peter Finch and Luke Wright.

A must for Dylan fans and poetry readers alike.

£9.99pbk. ISBN 9781854115607

SEREN

Well chosen words

Seren is an independent publisher with a wide-ranging list which includes poetry, fiction, biography, art, translation, criticism and history. Many of our books and authors have been shortlisted for – or won – major literary prizes, among them the Costa Award, the Man Booker, Forward Prize, and TS Eliot Prize.

At the heart of our list is a good story told well or an idea or history presented interestingly or provocatively. We're international in authorship and readership though our roots are here in Wales (Seren means Star in Welsh), where we prove that writers from a small country with an intricate culture have a worldwide relevance.

Our aim is to publish work of the highest literary and artistic merit that also succeeds commercially in a competitive, fast changing environment. You can help us achieve this goal by reading more of our books – available from all good bookshops and increasingly as e-books. You can also buy them at 20% discount from our website, and get monthly updates about forthcoming titles, readings, launches and other news about Seren and the authors we publish.

www.serenbooks.com